T0081420

Special Diets

Nut-Free Diets

by Mari Schuh

Consulting Editor: Gail Saunders-Smith, PhD

Consultant:
Amy L. Lusk, MS, RD, LD
Registered Dietitian

CAPSTONE PRESS
a capstone imprint

Pebble Plus is published by Capstone Press,
1710 Roe Crest Drive, North Mankato, Minnesota 56003.
www.capstonepub.com

Library of Congress Cataloging-in-Publication Data
Schuh, Mari C., 1975–
Nut-free diets / by Mari Schuh
     pages cm.— (Pebble plus. Special diets)
Audience: Age 4-8.
Audience: Grades K to 3.
ISBN 978-1-4914-0591-8 (library binding)
ISBN 978-1-4914-6584-4 (paperback)
ISBN 978-1-4914-0625-0 (eBook pdf)
1. Food allergy—Diet therapy—Juvenile literature. 2. Nut-free diet—Recipes—Juvenile literature. I. Title.
 RC588.D53N88 2015
 641.5′6318—dc23
                                   2014001857

Editorial Credits
Shelly Lyons, editor; Heidi Thompson, designer; Kelly Garvin, media researcher;
    Katy LaVigne, production specialist

Photo Credits
Capstone Studio/Karon Dubke, cover, cover insets, 7, 9, 11, 13, 15, 17, 19, 21, 22; Shutterstock/Tyler Olson, 5

Note to Parents and Teachers

The Special Diets series supports national science standards related to health and nutrition. This book describes and illustrates some foods that fit and don't fit into a nut-free diet. The images support early readers in understanding the text. The repetition of words and phrases helps early readers learn new words. This book also introduces early readers to subject-specific vocabulary words, which are defined in the Glossary section. Early readers may need assistance to read some words and to use the Table of Contents, Glossary, Read More, Internet Sites, and Index sections of the book.

Printed in the United States of America in Eau Claire, Wisconsin.
031519   001762

Table of Contents

Who Needs a Nut-Free Diet?

Do you know anyone with a nut allergy? People with nut allergies must avoid nuts. But they can eat many foods.

Eat This, Not That

Peanut butter is yummy.

Some kids can't eat it.

They can eat sunflower seed

butter instead. It's made

from sunflower seeds.

Ice cream is often made

in places with nuts.

People can enjoy

a smoothie instead.

It's made with fruit, ice, and juice.

Bakery items such as cookies and cakes can have nuts. Adults can make nut-free cookies and cakes at home. These foods are safe to eat.

People who can't eat nuts
can still enjoy other healthy foods.
They can eat vegetables and fruits.
Carrots and celery make
healthy snacks.

A lot of foods have nuts in them.
Adults who know about
food allergies can read food labels.
They can see what is safe.

What's a Reaction?

People with nut allergies

can have a reaction

if they eat or touch nuts.

They might throw up or get hives.

They may have a hard time breathing.

When people have
an allergic reaction,
they need medicine.
Tell an adult and
call 911 right away.

Be a Good Friend

Kids who are allergic to
peanuts and nuts might bring
their own food to school.
Be nice and don't tease.
After snack time everyone
can play together.

Safe Recipe
Very Berry Smoothie

What You Need

1 cup (240 mL) cranberry juice
1 cup (240 mL) milk
2 cups (480 mL) frozen berries,
   such as strawberries, blueberries,
   or raspberries
2 tbsp. (30 mL) honey (optional)

What You Do

Put all ingredients in a blender.
Mix at high speed for one minute.
Enjoy a smooth berry smoothie.

Makes 5 cups

Glossary

allergic—when something, like food or a bee sting, makes someone feel very sick

allergic reaction—the body's response when a person with a food allergy breathes in, touches, or eats a certain food; a reaction may cause an upset stomach, hives, breathing problems, and other problems

food allergy—a condition that makes people very sick when they breathe in, touch, or eat a certain food

hive—an itchy spot or red patch on the skin caused by an allergy or illness

label—a list on food wrappers that shows what the food is made of

Read More

Landau, Elaine. *Food Allergies. Head-to-Toe Health*. Tarrytown, N.Y.: Marshall Cavendish Benchmark, 2010.

Olson, Gillia M. *MyPlate and You*. Health and Your Body. Mankato, Minn.: Capstone Press, 2012.

Wethington, Julie. *Yes I Can!: Have My Cake and Food Allergies Too*. Columbia, MD: DragonWing Books, 2012.

Internet Sites

FactHound offers a safe, fun way to find Internet sites related to this book. All of the sites on FactHound have been researched by our staff.

Here's all you do:
Visit *www.facthound.com*
Type in this code: 9781491405918

Super-cool stuff! Check out projects, games and lots more at
www.capstonekids.com

Index

Critical Thinking Using the Common Core

1. Healthy foods are an important part of a nut-free diet. What are some healthy foods that you can include in your diet? (Key Ideas and Details)

2. Some people are allergic to nuts. If you see someone having an allergic reaction, what should you do? (Key Ideas and Details)

Word Count: 208
Grade: 1
Early-Intervention Level: 16

24